CAREER AND ROMANCE

How To Find Your
Soul Mate *As A*
Single Career Professional

EPHRAIM UNUIGBE

Career & Romance

How to Find Your Soul Mate as a Single Career Professional

Ephraim Unuigbe

Copyright 2022 © **Ephraim Unuigbe**

All rights reserved.

No part of this book may be reproduced, distributed, stored, or transmitted in any form or by any means, including electronic, photocopy, recording, copying, or resale, without the prior written permission of the author and publisher, except in the case of brief quotations embodied in reviews and articles as well as specific other non-commercial uses permitted by copyright law.

Contact the author via info@ephraim-unuigbe.online; ephraim.unuigbe@gmail.com

DEDICATION

I dedicate this book to my lovely wife – Marian Uzoma Unuigbe.

TABLE OF CONTENTS

Dedication

Preface

Chapter 1: Get to Know People First Before Trying to Marry Them.........12

Chapter 2: Go with The Right Motive................................24

Chapter 3: Use Your Network ……………………………………...41

Chapter 4: Be Visible Online ……………………………………….52

Chapter 5: Go On Dates in The Open ...…………………………...66

Chapter 6: Have an Open Mind.......................................77

Chapter 7: Do You Really Want or Need a Spouse...............89

About The Book………………………………………………...100

About The Author……………………………………………....101

Acknowledgments……………………………………………...103

Other Books by the Author to date…..................................104

Services We Offer………………………………………………105

PREFACE

As per a report on StatisticsTimes.com, as of 2021, there were 3,970,238,390 or 3,970 million or 3.97 billion males in the world, representing 50.42% of the world's population. It is estimated that there are 3,904,727,342 females in the world, or 3,905 million or 3.905 billion females, representing 49.58% of the world's population. The number of males worldwide is 65,511,048, or 65.51 million more than females.

Additionally, the report states that the gender ratio in the world will be 101.68 males per 100 females in 2021. The number of females was more significant than r of males until 1957. It is estimated that the ratio of males to females worldwide has increased from 99.692 in 1950 to at most 101.704 in 2011. There is now an expectation that it will decline to 100.296 by 2100.

In many countries and regions worldwide, there are more females than males. In contrast, the two most populous countries, China and India, have a significantly higher male population. There are, therefore, more males in the world than females. Taking China and India out of the picture, there are more females than males in the rest of the world.

It is a general belief that the number of women is more significant than, but as you may have deduced from the above, there are enough males to go around for every female. Therefore, except if you live in India or China, your chance of landing a spouse is higher overall as a male. This is in no way suggesting that if you are based in these two countries mentioned, it will be more complex; it's to analyze these numbers further and give you a broader perspective.

And if you checked the statistics and observed that the percentage of the opposite gender is lower in your country, which reduces your chances of getting a spouse there, you can relocate to another country to get a spouse, and it is easier now on the internet age. It is the same way as landing a job in a different country, so do not let a geographical limitation be why you are not looking. The world has become one global village, and almost anything is possible.

I am aware that it may be more challenging than it sounds because of other considerations to examine before deciding if taking a spouse from another country may be suitable for you. This is why the first chapter of the book centers on getting to know people first before trying to marry Them! Then, we discuss going in with the right mindset, and so on.

The search for a spouse can be overwhelming for some people. It may become even more challenging for career professionals to balance various aspects of their lives, such as attending to demanding workloads, managing their finances, and juggling friends and family obligations. The purpose of this book is to assist you in selecting the right spouse for yourself.

Toward the end of the book, you are encouraged to ask whether you really need a spouse. There is an excellent reason to ask this question in this time and age as many people search to satisfy the pressure from society. However, when you do not have a compelling reason for wanting a spouse in the first place, the search for one may become a distraction from your goals. Additionally, I discussed some reasons why some people wish to avoid being married and how to approach the issue if this is what you prefer.

As you can imagine, this book is packed with handy tips to help you decide and should be a handy companion for yourself and others you may know who may be having difficulties finding love.

Career
&
Romance

How to Find Your Soul Mate as a Single Career Professional

Get To Know People First Before Trying to Marry Them

CHAPTER ONE

GET TO KNOW PEOPLE FIRST BEFORE TRYING TO MARRY THEM

It has been observed that most single people of marriageable age tend to think about getting married rather than developing friendships, and they end up with strangers after the wedding. Although this may seem obvious, getting to know someone before initiating marriage conversations is always more advantageous for you in the long run.

The complexity of human beings makes it impossible to begin to understand them in a few days, weeks, or even months. Examine your circle of genuine friends to determine how long you have known them and how long it has taken you to become acquainted with them. If you are honest, you will realize that getting to know them took quite some time and that you still do not know everything about them. If you apply the same logic to someone you plan to spend the rest of your life with, you will realize you need time to get to know them.

Indeed, there is always an exception to the rule, such as when you meet someone for the first time and feel an immediate connection with them. However, even though this may be true in terms of conversations with them and comfort around them, there is a great deal of another background, personal, and family information that you do not know and can only learn once you spend time building a relationship with them. For example, I recall hearing the story of a man who discovered many years later that his wife did not graduate from college. Of course, this is a deal-breaker for him, and the lady acts as if she is a graduate to gain his acceptance.

However, I also realize that no matter how long a person tries to build a relationship with a person, there can never be a guarantee that they know everything about that person before marriage. There may be several reasons for this, including a good pretender who wants to get a favour, the fact that there are too many things to keep track of, or the conversation never coming up. In any case, what is essential is to take time into marriage. Instead, take your time to get to know them until you are entirely convinced and feel a sense of peace.

There is a good chance that something is not suitable if you feel in your mind that all is not well. It is not advisable to proceed at this point. You should not proceed with a decision if you feel uneasy about it. Again, you should only proceed if you feel a connection to the person. Be careful not to rush into saying yes or feel under pressure. It is unnecessary to run into a marriage that is expected to last forever. Don't let society, your friends, or your family pressure you into doing something you will regret.

How long is enough

You probably expect me to provide you with a timeframe, but I apologize for disappointing you. As far as the time frame is concerned, there is none. If you carefully read and understand the last paragraph, you will already know how long it takes to become familiar with someone.

You will be able to extract as much information as you wish based on the amount of time you spend with the person, the content of your conversations with the person, and what activities you engage in with them. Therefore, you should be deliberate about the points mentioned in this chapter and prepare a plan around them in order to maximize every opportunity you have to speak with them.

It would be best if you were sincere regarding the time needed. The key is to be open and deliberate when building a friendship that will last a lifetime. If you want to develop a friendship for a lifetime, how long should I allow? The answer to that question will determine how long it is enough and what will drive the relationship.

A checklist of things to know about people

Some points here may appear trivial or humorous, but trust me, they are essential. You do not need to worry about whether the topics on this checklist are necessary; ask so you will not be surprised later.

- Ask them for their full name and their real name. Find out if they have changed their names previously or if a particular name has known them in the past. You may want to obtain some evidence, such as certification, if possible.

- it is advisable to ask them about their educational background with some supporting evidence. I gave an example of how things could go wrong without this information

- Ask them what they do for a living. It is not uncommon for some people to have married fraudsters or individuals involved in illegitimate trades or businesses. If you discover the problem later, it may be too late.

- Obtain information about the family background of the individual. Providing information such as their parents' names, their siblings, and their upbringing would be helpful. This knowledge will enable you to treat and relate to them more effectively later in life. Let me take a quick diversion here. It is highly doubtful you'll be able to change someone successfully. Therefore, if you suspect there is something, you should act immediately.

- Make sure you ask about their relationship status and whether they have children from previous relationships. Although surprisingly, they may not be aware that they have one, it would be worthwhile to find out.

- Find out about their medical history. For example, if they have a family history of mental health issues, inquire whether they have ever suffered from it. Find out their genotype and blood group. You may also want to ask about any general health issues in the family and if there have been any terminal illnesses in the past.

- Inquire about the mentors and role models they look up to. By doing so, you will better understand their motivations and the type of future they will have. In other words, if they are only wealthy, people only surround them will also become rich, and the opposite is also true. Additionally, if they listen to admirable and positive people in society, they will eventually succeed.

- Find out what they think about divorce and other family-related topics.

- As well as observing their money habits, ask them about their spending habits. For example, find out if they have ever had debt in the past or if they are currently in debt. From their behavior, you will be able to learn more about their approach to money if you take the time to get to know them. For some insight, I recommend you obtain a copy of my previous book, **Managing Family Finance.**

Please note that these points are only intended as a guide. Nothing is set in stone. Be flexible, and don't be rigid in your approach. There is no expectation that you will get the answer to all the questions in one go. Sometimes, a person will deliberately provide you with the answer you want to hear. Therefore, you should apply wisdom as you embark on this journey of getting to know others. You may not need to ask some of these questions since they will likely come up during conversations. I would also like that you refrain from making a list of these questions. Be guided by wisdom.

The checklist will help you determine whether or not you are compatible based on the answers you receive to these questions. By doing so, you will be able to show whether you wish to proceed or not. Additionally, the response will determine whether further inquiries are necessary.

It is possible to receive all positive responses to these questions, but somewhere in your mind, you know something is wrong. I have already mentioned that if your gut feeling does not align with your hearing, you should follow that feeling.

Some people may not be suitable for you as a spouse, but they are still excellent friends. Consequently, only dismiss people if they meet your criteria for marriage. There is still a possibility that they would be valuable allies (allies with mutual benefits). A good friend is not necessarily a good match for you.

Chapter One Summary

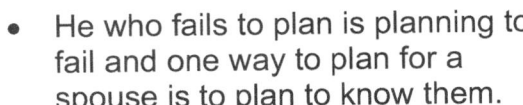

- He who fails to plan is planning to fail and one way to plan for a spouse is to plan to know them.

- Humans can be deceptive and knowing them may require more time than anticipated.

- There are some basic questions that you need to ask. Take your time.

- There is really no one size fits all. You will know what is important for you.

- Always, always follow your heart and listen to your instinct.

GO WITH THE RIGHT MOTIVE

CHAPTER TWO

GO WITH THE RIGHT MOTIVE

Do you have a particular reason for wanting to be married? Is there a specific reason why? Does it have anything to do with your age or that all your friends are married? Perhaps you feel you have become too old? Is it because your parents want you to move out or because of social pressure? Does it have to do with your desire to paint the town red? Perhaps you are motivated by what you see on social media. Maybe several flamboyant wedding trains and beautiful dresses have been presented to you, or Jim and Pam's wedding inspired you in The Office show, and you want to recreate it? It may also be that you wish to escape your current financial circumstances or that marriage will make you wealthy.

Having any of the above reasons is not a good reason to get married. The mere fact that you are now 40 is not enough to justify your marriage. You cannot rely solely on the fact that all of your friends are married.

There are several legitimate reasons for wanting to get married, and this chapter will provide information to help redirect your thinking.

Some Good Reasons to Get Married

- **Companionship**

    A companion, by dictionary definition, is –

    a person or animal with whom

    one spends much time with

    whom one travels.

    Of course, we are referring to a person here. Another definition:

    Companion is defined as each of a

    pair of things intended to complement

or match each other.

It is clear from these definitions that three keywords can be derived: *travel*, *time*, and *complement*.

There are many ups and downs in life. The challenges you will face will be numerous, and it would be beneficial to have someone to turn to when you return home to diffuse some negative energy. Therefore, the travel component of the definition is described here.

In the context of time, it is evident that you intend to live a long time. You would surely want to be able to share that moment with someone if you were to live for 100 years on this earth. You should not have many memories you cannot communicate with those you hold close to your heart. We all want to make many memories that will last a lifetime, and it is natural for humans to wish to share those memories with others.

The complement bit of the definition refers to having someone who will gain an advantage in areas where you may be deficient. For example, you will inevitably grow old and tired, so I assume you would like to live an efficient and practical life. As a result, you should hone in on your strengths while utilizing the strengths of someone who can assist you in other areas of your life where you are deficient and share your strengths.

As you may have already observed, life's journey is better enjoyed by a companion. The wish is an innate one that somehow fulfills the individual's desires. There is a need that another individual can only meet.

- **Helper**

There is a close relationship between this and companionship, but the two are not identical. The term "helper" refers to someone who can perform tasks you cannot complete and is not necessarily something you are not interested in. Compliment involves helping you with things you need help understanding or need more time to do, while a helper assists you with something you cannot do on your own.

There will inevitably be many things in life that you will not be able to accomplish, even with all your time. Even though money may be able to meet these needs, it does not convey the same feeling as having someone close to take care of them for you. The satisfaction you experience from getting a loved one to do something for you cannot be matched by any confidentiality agreement or a non-disclosure agreement.

It's worth mentioning that as you gather your answers to the questions raised in chapter one, you should look for someone who will complement and help you. If the person does the same thing, you may want to look for someone else. Ideally, it would be best if you married someone who does not do something similar to what you do or what you are good at.

Naturally, opposites attract. So, you are more likely to be drawn to someone entirely different from yourself. Someone that has something you lack. Although you are aware of your actions and know why you are attracted or drawn to this person, being deliberate about it gives you an advantage as you are now conscious of your actions.

- **Children**

One of the many reasons why people want to get married is to have a child. I know many have children without being married through different means, but here we're focusing on why you want to get married, not why you should get married. The reason you wish not to have children is valid if that is your motivation.

The legacy you leave behind is extended through your children. This is a natural way to live your life through another individual. You will likely wish to have a child that will carry on your wealth and name if you are or plan to be wealthy in the future. Having your children is a fantastic way to do this.

There is no doubt that your child may be the most reliable person to entrust your resources to, and they are someone you can trust to continue doing what is important to you in the future.

It is possible to literally "build" a different individual from scratch, instilling only the best elements into them, and expect them to continue to make a positive impact on the world after they leave you. If this is your motivation for having children and getting married, then you are on the right track.

How To Know You Are Ready

It may not be the right time to get married, even if you know all the good reasons to do so. So, in order to understand whether you are ready, what should you look out for in yourself? I have outlined five criteria below.

Financially

Is it true that you do not have any money but wish to get married? Perhaps you are only somewhat comfortable from a financial standpoint. Please do not feel pressured into getting married when you are not financially ready, and I hope things will be fine. Obviously, if you intend to construct a house, you will consider the associated costs. This is similar to the process of building a family. No matter who you are, whether you are a woman or a man, you still need money.

Although there are some exceptions to the rule, marriage should not be used to escape financial difficulties. Instead, in light of what has been stated previously, it should be for much deeper reasons.

Financial security is not determined by the amount of money you earn but by matching your current needs with your current income. A person is only ready if they can meet their own needs.

Emotionally

The importance of emotional maturity cannot be overstated. Throughout your life, you will share personal space with a "stranger" who will become your spouse. It is important to note that this individual may come from a completely different background and experience of what an ideal family entails. In addition to life issues, family planning, television programs, career focuses, child upbringing, and other topics, they also have opinions on different matters.

Your views on many issues may differ significantly. Several times a day, you will have to compromise. How will you respond when this person deliberately annoys you? Do you know how to love yourself if no one else does? Are your self-confidence and self-acceptance high?

Love is one of the characteristics of emotional maturity. First, love yourself, and then you can love others. In love, it is not about what you receive but about what you give. As a result, it is possible to give someone so much love that they do not reciprocate with the same amount of love. How would you respond if this were your situation?

No one expects you to be perfect and to have everything figured out. I am only preparing your mind to understand the height of emotional maturity. The Internet provides a variety of books and videos that can be viewed in order to learn how to become more mature emotionally. The key to learning is to implement, not to read or watch. Wisdom comes from doing.

Spiritually

This is a topic that I discussed in my previous book, How to Choose a Career Path. You will need to be spiritually mature to cope with many situations in life. The lack of spiritual intelligence is dangerous. There are many unforeseen circumstances that one can escape when they are spiritually intelligent.

Spirituality is the force that binds all other ends together. Therefore, even if one is prepared financially, physically, emotionally, and in every other way, there are still many loopholes that one might have yet to consider. Being spiritually enlightened covers this aspect.

Physical events in life are controlled from a spiritual perspective. Therefore, it would be naïve to think that spirituality does not exist. Sometimes, one can only pray; if you haven't figured it out spiritually, life may become even more challenging.

Physically

In this regard, you should consider how comfortable you are with your physical appearance. Do you feel satisfied with the way you look? Is there anything you can do about it? If you are able to do so, please do so. The best thing you can do is to learn to live with it if you cannot change it.

In no way does this have anything to do with whether or not you are beautiful. The truth is that everyone is beautiful, depending on who is looking at them. As the popular saying goes, "beauty is in the eye of the beholder." Do not allow anyone to tell you that you are not beautiful. There will be someone somewhere who likes the way you look.

Physical hygiene is also included in the term physical. Do you need to start applying roll-on? Have you been taking a bath every day? How often do you brush your teeth? Is your underwear in good condition? According to a popular saying, "cleanliness is next to godliness." This statement is also true. Being physically clean can always stay in fashion.

Physically also pertains to your current residence. For example, does your house need to be cleaned? You do not have to clean it yourself; you can hire someone to do it for you and your laundry. I am sure you get the idea.

Other Aspect

There are various soft skills you can assess yourself on that will be relevant and valuable for a marriage relationship, including intellectual preparation and other soft skills. In addition, it may be worthwhile to speak with more experienced married individuals around you.

You do not need to worry about whether they are happily married; what you ask is what their experience has been, what they can advise, and what you can learn from their experience. As a wise person, you are able to distinguish between what is right and what is wrong based on what you are told.

While you are in the process of finding a spouse, why not develop some of your shortcomings? The preparation you undertake while you wait will enable you to be adequately prepared.

Chapter Two Summary

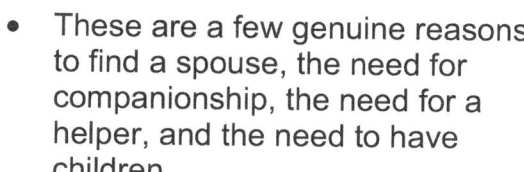

- These are a few genuine reasons to find a spouse, the need for companionship, the need for a helper, and the need to have children.

- You can know you are ready for companionship if you are matured financially, emotionally, spiritually, and physically.

- Marriage is not a rehabilitation center, therefore, don't go in with an expectation for one person to meet all your needs. Don't also expect to change people when you get in.

- Review your own reasons for wanting a spouse. Are they genuine enough?

- Do you think you are ready, or do you need to work more on yourself?

Use Your Network

CHAPTER THREE

USE YOUR NETWORK

Are you a member of any physical or social networks? Do you think volunteering in your local community society would be an excellent way to expand your network? You will likely miss meeting new people while you are locked up in your However, there are many for you to meet new people, so you need to be out there getting in touch with them.

You may be able to meet people through your current network, but if you are not visible in those networks and no one knows about you, you may not be taking advantage of all the resources.

If you know married people around you whom you admire for their marriages, you should ask for recommendations. No one should feel ashamed about these things; some people have a more challenging time finding a spouse than others, so they will understand why you ask.

Some Ways to Get Optimum Results from Your Network

- **Ask how you can help**

    Those active in local gatherings tend to be more recognized and have access to a broader audience. You will have the opportunity to show many people the quality of your character, and they will be able to come to know and appreciate you.

    If you belong to a community and are not participating in any activity or helping, you are causing yourself more harm than good. While it may appear that you are doing someone a favour by helping out, the truth is that you are contributing to your well-being.

- **Stay in touch**

    If you are a member of a local church, club, or any other local gathering, it is best to stay in touch by regularly attending meetings and other events. Someone else may observe your attendance and commitment to the discussions to decide which person they would like to date.

- **Connect your contacts**

    Along with keeping in touch and helping, you can also serve as a resource and connector of people. It is natural for everyone to enjoy being served, and people always remember those who assisted them at a particular point in their lives.

    As the saying goes, a good turn deserves another. So your motive for doing these things should not be because you are looking for a spouse but rather because you are a good person.

- **Share your time and resources**

    Learn how to assist people in their daily activities and personal lives. Identify what you are good at and what you can do seamlessly, and volunteer to help others in that area.

- **Include and collaborate**

    Rather than competing with others, collaborate with them. Take a genuine interest in people. Wherever you are in the world, you will surely find strangers around you who don't look precisely like "your people." Be nice to them. You can be recommended to your spouse by strangers. How you treat strangers may be the deciding factor for someone interested in you.

- **Pick up the phone**

    Be sure to check in on people. You may know an older man or woman in your community who does not have anyone to assist them. Please call them now and then and brighten their day. These individuals will likely be able to provide you with positive reviews and recommendations.

- **Be nice to people you consider less than you**

    Realistically, no one is less than you; they are not yet in their season. For this reason, you see people who may appear below you make tremendous progress within a short period.

We all experience these times and seasons from time to time, so you should treat everyone with dignity and respect at all times. Not just because of what they can be but because it is the right thing to do. In the end, it does not matter whether or not they make tremendous progress.

- **Show Appreciation**

    Appreciation is something that everyone enjoys. When you show your appreciation to someone, it may not immediately be acknowledged; however, it sticks in their minds. Their eyes will light up when they see how much you appreciate what they did for you, however small it may seem.

    When you show gratitude and appreciation to someone, regardless of whether they are essential, you have done your part to strengthen your relationship and network.

- **Be vulnerable**

My first published book, Succeeding in Your Career, explains why this could be a positive quality. Everyone has weaknesses, and everyone will display this at some point. As you realize this in yourself, note that it is not the weakness that poses the problem but what you do about it and how you handle it.

Occasionally, it may be necessary to allow yourself to be vulnerable instead of portraying yourself as a superhuman; after all, you are not a superhero. Being vulnerable will enable people to see you for who you are, the real you, and helps prevent multiple personalities from emerging. As a result, you may always find that you continually explain yourself to people unnecessarily, and you could lose your value. Authentic individuals are liked and appreciated by others. Therefore, it is essential that you remain true to yourself and everyone around you.

- **Do not always be right**

Being in this position is a difficult situation for most people. People are usually inclined to believe that they are right most of the time. It gives them a sense of fulfillment and makes them feel good about themselves. There are times when you can be right and remain silent. There are times when you may have the correct answer and stay quiet. Individuals who possess this level of emotional intelligence are considered mature. You will have your chance to share what you know.

Sometimes, let people have their way, allow them to shine, and will enable them to feel good. However, you should occasionally be concerned with winning and having all the correct answers and ideas. Developing relationships takes time, and that time is shortened when you show a genuine interest in those you interact with and their happiness. One way to demonstrate this is to allow them to have their way, even if they are incorrect.

Chapter Three Summary

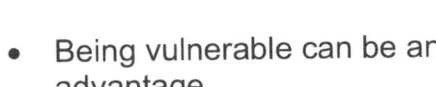

- Being vulnerable can be an advantage.

- Be a continuous learner, you will not always be right.

- Being nice tells more of who you are rather than the people you are being nice to.

- Be a genuinely nice person not because of what you stand to gain.

- Pick up your phone and call people. Stay in touch and be available.

Be Visible Online

CHAPTER FOUR

BE VISIBLE ONLINE

If you seek a life partner but no one knows about it, how can we be sure that you are looking? Or are you seeking a spouse on social media, but your page is private? Of course, it is also possible that you need to be online. Or the Instagram platform does not appeal to you; it is just not your style. The truth is that you should be available and appear to be available online so that people will get to know you and be able to reach out to you.

It is the internet age, and things have changed a bit. Compared to the 90s and early 20s, the methods that worked then no longer work as effectively. This serves as a wake-up call if you are not active online and must adapt to the changing times. This applies not only to dating but to every aspect of life.

It will be necessary for you, if you are a lady, to be out there and available, and if you are a man, you will need to be out there and look. It is almost impossible to live efficiently and effectively in the 21st century without access to the internet. This will isolate you from the rest of the world. Therefore, it is okay to use dating apps if you do so in a safe manner.

In your current circle, there is a possibility that you will not meet your spouse. As part of your job search, you may need to engage in other activities and use online platforms. In projecting yourself here, you are not necessarily telling people that you are seeking a spouse or partner; instead, you are taking advantage of this forum to network and form friendships and relationships with other members and eventually find a spouse. In general, this order should be followed.

The first question to answer is whether you are on social media. It is optional for you to be present on all platforms; you are free to choose the one(s) that are most comfortable. There are several popular social networking sites, to choosing Twitter, Instagram, and Facebook. In addition to these, several other sites may not appear to be for dating, but from which you can still build valuable relationships, such as TikTok, YouTube, Clubhouse, LinkedIn, and a variety of other sites. Then, there are the popular dating apps - Bumble, Tinder, OkCupid, Match, Grindr, eHarmony, etc. Please remain safe when using these apps. Be cautious when using these platforms.

The next question is, how often do you update and post on social media? It is not enough to be present on these platforms; you must also actively participate and create content on them. Visibility is determined by the quality of your creations and contributions and not simply by the content you consume. It is possible to be online for many years and only gain something tangible if you consume content. As mentioned earlier, relationships require two-way communication, a give-

and-take situation, so if you are only taking without giving, many people will consider you a friend.

You do not have to create content every day or every week, but you must be consistent with your efforts. You can choose a platform and a message and then contribute regularly. For example, several weeks ago, I began posting about career and personal finance on my LinkedIn profile every Tuesday. It is clear that I am not looking for a spouse but to build valuable connections and relationships and give back to the next generation. Please choose a suitable platform, be comfortable with it, and maintain consistency.

How To Build a Valuable Online Presence

- **Use video**

    There should be no doubt about this. People are always curious to know who is behind the message. This is why, while driving on a motorway, if a driver drives badly from what you would expect, once you have overtaken them, you may glance at their face again. As for you, it does not have to be related to your behaviour but rather to the quality and the type of content you post.

Even though the intention is not to use video just for the sake of it in your search for a spouse, but rather be visible with video posts to demonstrate who you are and how you look.

It is essential, however, to do just what is necessary. There are different platforms for different types of content, so posting too many videos on LinkedIn, for example, may not be advisable. The use of video on this platform should be limited. Most videos are uploaded to

YouTube, short videos to Instagram, and even shorter videos to TikTok.

It's advisable to maintain a decent appearance while using videos. Using videos allows people to see other forms of communication you make with your body language and appearance that you couldn't express with words. You can also communicate using your body language while using videos. You can find many articles and teachings online that explain how to use gestures properly.

- **Include your contacts in things you post online.**

Have you identified your platform for content creation yet? Then the next thing you can do is to let your contacts see what you post online. Even if you are not active on those platforms where your contacts are, it helps many people to see you as you create more awareness of your unique personality. Then, you can screenshot your posts and share them on other platforms.

This is important because only some in your contact list are on all the platforms you are on. So sharing helps expand your influence and unique personality. In addition, this creates an avenue for you to have conversations and build a community – connection – relationship – spouse.

- **Customize your outgoing message**
  If you have to send people Direct Messages (DMs), make the messages more personal by customizing them. Do not use a bland and generic message. Also, do not sound entitled to information from others when sending a DM. or

make it feel like you are doing them a favour by sending them a message.

When making a connection on LinkedIn, for example, do not just click on "connect." Instead, there is an option to add a customized message to that connection invite; use it to tell the person you are connecting to why you are connecting with them. This is an opportunity to send a direct and more personal message than a random connection. This is also an opportunity to be more deliberate about building relationships.

- **Stay connected**

  As with every other avenue for building relationships, you are staying in touch is the key to establishing a more personal relationship online. It is not enough to claim to know somebody if you have not taken the time to develop a relationship with them. Considering that you are trying to find a spouse, this is especially important. It is not only because you are seeking a spouse that you have noticed potential in these individuals you are connected to, but also because you wish to build a relationship with them.

As this process will take time, you need to be patient and not make it awkward by being too available. You should be deliberate in your approach and take the time to get to know them, their values, their strengths, and what initially attracted you to them.

- **Slow down**

    Take your time and keep building. The journey to building a relationship is a marathon and not a sprint. Desperation tends to drive our desire for instant results and success, but one cannot make this process faster with this attitude.

It would be best if you slowed down again because anything that will last the test of time takes time to build. One of chapter two's emphases was going in with the right mindset. You may want to reread it.

- **Engage and be helpful**

You do not always have to be the original poster of the content. In some situations, you can contribute your thoughts to other people's content by engaging with their posts. Even if no one reads it immediately, someone might see it someday and start a conversation. A simple conversation can lead to a connection, which leads to a relationship, and a relationship can lead to marriage.

Help people online. There is always one person that asks obvious questions they can get answers to if they use Google. Please help them. Help them find the answer if you do not have one. There is a solution to every problem.

Choosing to help those in need is going to take much work every time. One thing to remember is to not be arrogant in your efforts to help those in need. You can also help them anonymously. You do not always have to blow your trumpet to make a difference. The fact that you have helped someone, and they are satisfied, can be enough reward for your selflessness. Furthermore, it will improve and strengthen your sense of morality.

- **Use different photos for your dating profile**
  You are not a statue! Although a picture may be worth a thousand words, it needs to provide more information about you, your traits, and your personality. Also, as much as it lies within your power, make your face consistent. Different

profile photos do not mean you constantly change your appearance.

This may need to be clarified for potential suitors. This also does not mean you must post and change your photos too frequently. There is a need to have a balance.

Chapter Four Summary

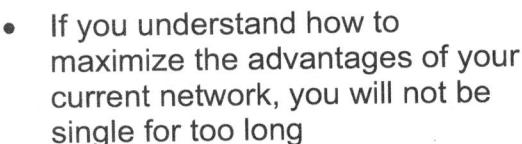

- If you understand how to maximize the advantages of your current network, you will not be single for too long

- You may need to be more visible online in this day and age to leave the "singles" room.

- Be open to learn new ways of doing things even though they may seem uncomfortable initially.

- It's okay to use dating apps

- When last did you change your profile picture?

Go On Dates in The Open

CHAPTER FIVE
GO ON DATES IN THE OPEN

There are a lot of unreasonable and wicked people in the world. These people can be found both online and offline. Some of these people have the primary objective of being online to hurt or swindle others. Therefore, do not suspend caution because you only interact with other people online.

In financial audit, the term professional skepticism refers to an attitude of doubt or the disposition towards incredulity that is present either in general or towards specific individuals. Until you have met someone personally or received a recommendation from someone you trust and know, put this cap on and be skeptical. If you do not know someone well, it is impossible to be too skeptical of them. It would be best if you considered everyone a potential suspect until some evidence is found to the contrary. Please do not overdo it. Trust your instincts; you will know what to do.

If you have to go on dates with someone you don't really know, meet them in an open place. Do not go on dates in people's homes if you do not know them very well. There is no difference whether you are a male or a female; the risks are the same. Although they may live in beautiful neighborhoods or own fancy houses or exotic cars, this is not a guarantee that they are good people.

Do not let your greed or desperation drive your actions. Instead, think critically and do your due diligence before agreeing to go on a date. You may suggest the rendezvous instead for your safety. Be convinced and comfortable before deciding to move forward.

Dating safety tips

- **Avoid connecting with suspicious profiles**

    As mentioned earlier, most times, your instinct is correct. If you are suspicious about a person, what they've said about themselves or/and whom they portray to be, you are probably right. And it doesn't matter whether it is offline or online. Do not let their flashy lifestyle deceive you.

    More than half of the things you see online about people are unreal. Not just something, sometimes even the people are fake. Especially on some online dating platforms, you may need to speak with the people you think you are talking with. Certain people have managed to master the art of deception and can use other people's photos in their profiles to deceive unsuspecting and innocent people.

- **Check out your potential date on social media**

    You do not need to become a CAI or M15 to perform a background check on A potential date. A simple google search can reveal much about a person, background, and interests. This will help you determine if what they've said matches what you have seen online from your search.

    Be careful, as some of these swindlers have mastered cleansing their online presence only to show what they want you to see. If their online presence is too "clean" for their personality, that may be a red flag. If it is too good to be true, it probably is.

- **Block and report suspicious users**

    It would be best to keep some people on hold because perhaps something will change. But, no, nothing will change. So, please do not succumb to temptation once you have established that someone may be suspicious; block and report them. This helps the administrators of those platforms to take necessary actions to delete those accounts permanently.

I've often observed that when celebrities send me a friend request, it's a fake account. I ask myself, "Why would a celebrity want to send me a friend request?". I usually delete their invites and report those. It doesn't matter if they have thousands of followers; it becomes suspicious, especially if they are not verified.

- **Wait to Share Personal Information**
Don't be too much in a hurry to divulge very personal information about you or your family. As mentioned earlier, some people, especially

online, are there to hurt people, and a little information about you may be the missing piece they need to launch an attack.

It is not the length of time that should determine how much information you give but when you become more familiar with and trust the person. Some people can go as far as hanging around you for a very long time to get information. Your instinct will know these people, don't ignore your intuition.

- **Don't Respond to Requests for Financial Help**

Do not let your emotions get the better of you. If the first thing a person asks for from you after the initial introduction is financial assistance, they probably need to be genuine people. Asking for financial aid is a complicated request to make. Only suspicious people make these requests freely. Therefore, if someone whom you are not familiar with and you are sure they don't know you are comfortable to ask you, let your skepticism be heightened.

This does not suggest that you should not help people when they are genuinely in need. You can perform a quick background check to see how genuine they may be. It is worth suggesting that they use a public donation platform like GoFundMe. Their response to this request may be the answer you need to know whether they are genuine

- **Video chat before you meet up in person**

    This may seem obvious, but quite important. A suspicious person will give you a thousand reasons why they cannot have a video call. My suggestion will be that if you ask twice and get an excuse those two times, that's a red flag. Just count your loss and move on with your life. The fact that they make a video call with you is not enough to guarantee still. This should be another level of authentication before deciding or concluding if someone is genuine or not.

- **Be cybersecurity smart**
    - Protect Your Personal Information with Strong Passwords. You already know this; ensure you follow the instructions for using a strong password. You will find information online about what makes a strong password.
    - Be Careful About Wi-Fi. If you can afford it, avoid using public Wi-Fi altogether.
    - Pay Attention to Software Updates. Don't just click update. You may set automatic updates instead. Updates should be done via authorized applications only and not popups.
    - Make Sure Your Devices Are Secure. It may be essential to use fingerprint or face scanning technology.

- Use recommended apps only and not one someone online suggested. Even if you have to use their suggestion, check the reviews to ensure they are right for you.
- Avoid charging your devices in public. Reports have revealed that your devices can be hacked from public charging ports. If you must, be prepared to absorb the risk, as I'm not sure there is a way to know if those ports are safe. Alternatively, you can carry a power plug or conserve your power when you are out.

Chapter Five Summary

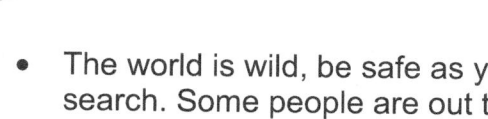

- The world is wild, be safe as you search. Some people are out to get you.

- Many things you see online are not real, don't be deceived.

- Following your instinct is always a smart move.

- Be discreet about the kind of personal information you share online

- Read up how to be safe online again.

Have an open mind

CHAPTER SIX
HAVE AN OPEN MIND

If you have followed through from chapter one to this chapter, you will realize that we have focused most of our discussions on what you can do and what to avoid. We have not mentioned anything about the kind of person you are looking for or anything like that. The focus should always be on what you can improve and what to change.

Once all have been rightly established, the right person will come along. This does not mean you must be 100% complete to meet the ideal man or woman; it just means you are working hard on yourself to be a good person, and that is all you can control.

In your search for the right partner, do not only rely on your list for the ideal man/woman; of course, but you should also have some criteria of perfect your ideal man/woman should be. Below we shall discuss a list of qualities an ideal man and woman should have.

The Ideal Partner

- **They are smart**

    This doesn't mean they must have a first-class from the university. On the contrary, they may not have attended university. There are different types or forms of smartness. Someone may be book-smart and not street-smart. Having an open mind helps you see through them to know what's right for you. If you are book smart, it may be better to have someone who is street smart.

    In my previous book, How to Choose a Career Path, I spoke extensively about discovering who you are. That book may help you understand your personality and what personality of the opposite sex will be the best match for you.

- **They make you laugh**

    This may be more of a female need, but you get the idea. Someone who makes you feel comfortable in your skin, someone you do not have to pretend to be someone else when around them.

    Ask yourself, are there things you cannot do when they are there? You may not have known them long enough and are not sure; that's different. You can tell from the onset if they are fun to be around or make you uncomfortable.

- **He actively supports your career**

    Is this person interested in your work or anything you do for money? I agree that some people may not be active in their support, but you will know they are in your corner and not against you. They are making your work manageable with their attitude.

Although this need is for both genders, it's more pronounced for women. Men generally may not want active support but still need help in other ways. The best you can do for your date if you can't actively support them is to encourage them to improve or suggest how they can improve on getting other suitable jobs.

- **They make an effort with their friends and family as you do with them.**

  Someone who wants you all to themselves is probably not the right person. Let me explain. The right person would like to show you off to their friends and family and would also like to meet yours.

  Note, however, that it may take some time for some people to take their time to be sure that you are right for them before they show you off. So you will know when it's time and when someone is stalling.

Please do not attempt to rush things to make them show you off on social media or introduce you to their friends and family. Someone with evil intent may set you up to satisfy this need if you insist.

If you are a male, be careful not to be too close to your partner's girlfriend. If you need anything from your girlfriend, ask your partner instead. It's the same if you are a female. There have been many stories of people who have violated this rule and regretted it later as they lost their partners in the process.

- **They are emotionally intelligent.**
Emotional intelligence is necessary for both parties, and I've,e dwelt extensively in the earlier chapter. We also spoke about physical, mental, and spiritual intelligence. Emotional intelligence

gives focus; physical intelligence gives quantity; cognitive intelligence gives quality; and spiritual intelligence provides purpose. A proper mix of these makes one fully mature and positions one for the right partner.

- **They respect your opinions and listen to what you have to say.**

  If you have gone out on several dates, you will know if they listen to you or are constantly interrupting. Are they always trying to shut you down and make you feel that your opinions are irrelevant in the conversation? Do they have all the best ideas, superimpose them on you, and not allow you to have a say? Do you feel intimidated when they speak and don't feel like talking after they have spoken, and they don't attempt to ask you what you think? If the answer to all of the questions is YES, they may not be suitable for you.

However, as mentioned earlier, don't conclude about someone just by this attitude but keep in mind that in any relationship, there is a need for communication. If it's one-way, that's not communication, and the relationship will not last very long. So both parties must be able and willing to have their say, whether right or wrong. Whether they make any sense or not.

- **They are willing to put the work in**

  What is the point of being in a relationship where you are the only one? As funny as this may sound, many people are dating themselves because they make all the effort and don't realize this is a dangerous signal. If you are the only party trying to ensure the relationship works, you are dating yourself.

  You will know when someone is trying to work on the relationship and commitment to its success. It is a severe red flag otherwise.

Another mistake people make is giving excuses for their partner's behaviour thinking they will change after marriage. I agree that people change over time, but it is a risk to hang your happiness on the fact that someone will change later.

- **They celebrate your achievements.**

Do they see you as a competition? This may be a red flag. There should be healthy competition between couples, especially if they are in the same line of work, to improve their quality and output. However, when it becomes like rivalry, it can degenerate into jealousy and envy and eventually sabotage.

Pay attention to the little things. Simple things like how they respond to your promotion at the office, how they react when you overcome a challenge, or when you fail at something, among others. Let your instinct guide you.

Tall, Dark, and Handsome

Other traits may be necessary to you, like a sense of style, how handsome or beautiful, height, muscular build, fitness, cooking, ability to clean, earning potential, passion (active enthusiasm in a pursuit), confidence, generosity, dependability, kindness, moral integrity, and fatherliness.

Generally, it is advisable to pay attention to your supposedly future spouse, their behaviour around you, and when you are not there. How you see them treat others, how they speak about others to you, and so on. Note these traits and decide if they fit into your ideal partner.

Notwithstanding, even if someone meets all the criteria above, it may still not be enough to conclude that they will be perfect for you. So I will emphasize again that you let your instinct guide you. Conversely, someone may only fit into some of your criteria and still be perfect. So be flexible and avoid boxing anyone into a strict list of criteria.

Perfection doesn't exist. Otherwise, no one will need to try. It takes two committed and hard-working individuals to make their lives and partnership work. While it's essential to make some allowance for their mistakes, you will know when someone is being deliberate in their behaviour or if they genuinely made a mistake. Tall, dark, and handsome every time only exist in the movies.

Chapter Six Summary

- Tall, dark, and handsome exist only in movies.

- There are more important criteria for selecting who is right for you, one is someone who is genuinely happy for you when you succeed.

- Being smart should be all encompassing, not just book smart.

- Will you marry yourself the way you are? As you search, look in the mirror and see if you like what you see.

- Your instinct works every time, make a habit to follow it.

Do You Really Want or Need a Spouse?

CHAPTER SEVEN

DO YOU REALLY WANT OR NEED A SPOUSE?

Many times, we want something because other people have it. Sometimes, we need to take a step back to examine ours wants to see how reasonable or necessary those wants are. This is critical when choosing a spouse. You do not need to have one. There are many examples of people that never got a spouse and were still thriving in their journey of life.

Before making this decision, there are a couple of thoughts to ponder, and this decision should not just be taken simply because your search has been unfruitful. Instead, it should be taken after carefully considering what you want for yourself and if you can manage to be alone. We shall examine being alone and lonely later in this chapter. But first, let's discuss why one may choose to be single.

Factors People Consider Being Single

Before delving into why people may choose to be single, it is essential to clarify what a single person is and is not in this context.

A single person is someone who chooses to be by themselves. Someone that is not in any relationship. This is not the same as friends-with-benefits arrangements, cohabiting with another person, or any of these funny arrangements we have these days. They decide not to be involved with anyone in the form of an intimate relationship. They do, however, have friends they hang out with without strings attached.

People that decide to be single consider all of the following amongst others, and these can also serve as advantages when choosing to be single

- People who are goal focused.

- People who perceive that they have traits that might interfere with attracting a prospective mate.
- People who view goal achievement as a strategy for choosing a spouse in the future
- People who want to have more choices of a spouse in the future
- People who do not want to feel under pressure
- People who do not want to be entangled with too many obligations
- People who prefer to maintain their freedom and space
- People who are in careers that require constant moving
- People who believe that there are many things they want to do in their lives that don't require a spouse.
- People who like the idea of being single

There are many reasons to be single, but it is also wrong if you choose to be single because you do not want to correct bad behaviour or excuses that can be worked on or fixed. Common examples in this category are.

- I am too old – nobody is too old to have a spouse. Someone out there is as old as you or even more senior, single, and looking for you!
- I am too selfish – this is probably the most selfish comment I've heard. However, selfishness is not a death sentence; you can work on it and be more selfless.
- Nobody likes me – I've stressed this enough in previous paragraphs. Love starts with you loving yourself first, and this helps you to manage expectations from others.
- I cannot live with someone – This is not true. You lived with your parents or someone at some point in your life. You can work on yourself to be more flexible and accommodating of others.

- I have experienced too many disappointments in the past. While this may be true, a little optimism can work wonders. You have often experienced disappointments in the past, but you still went ahead and did them anyway until you succeeded. I agree it is a bit different as this is a matter of the heart, but keep trying and adjust your strategies. This, too, will be like those other things
- I cannot have children – this is a genuine reason for concern but not a reason to be single. However, some people do not want children, too, so, as you can see, this is an advantage as it streamlines your search for a match!
- I have a disability – this is an even better reason to have a spouse. Many people are disabled and have spouses. Don't let this be your reason to remain single.
- I do not trust others easily – this character trait can be adjusted to the right amount of trust. Not trusting depends on positive characteristics in

the right situation. A level of skepticism is required in every relationship, which can be used as an advantage.

- Fear of failure – this is the core of love. A situation where you don't think of just yourself but also others. If you have the right amount of love, you will not have this fear. This is because you will trust yourself to put in the work from your side and hope that your spouse will hold up to their end of the rope. You will expect it because you love it. All fears can be conquered by the right amount of love.

- I am shy or cannot find someone interesting – we both know this is not true. You haven't searched enough. You may have tried but not enough. Give it another go and another go until you get your desired result. Like everything else, you cannot simply give in because you have met an obstacle. It would be best if you kept trying until you got your desires

Single People Whom You Should Know

- Queen Elizabeth I
- Isaac Newton
- Florence Nightingale
- Nikola Tesla
- Condoleezza Rice
- Hans Christian Andersen
- Diane Keaton
- The Wright Brothers
- Jon Hamm
- Louisa May Alcott

Alone and Lonely

Being alone should not be confused with being lonely. These two words communicate different ideas. Someone can be isolated and be fulfilled because they are focused on their goals and still share life's experiences with general friends and family. On the other hand, someone who chooses to be alone will need to have a full grasp of their purpose in life and what they want to achieve, and mingling with relationships may not be in their best interest then. Being alone can also be a temporary phase of a person's life.

On the other hand, people can be lonely even if they have a spouse. Being lonely is a state of mind and not a factor of people around them. Factors primarily responsible for loneliness can result from low self-worth and a feeling of being unloved. These categories of people fail to understand that happiness and fulfillment are not a function of external factors or material things acquired but more of what they think of themselves and the effort they make to be better people, as well as understanding that there are many things that they do not have control over. These people need to understand that self-love is the most important thing on this life journey. Once there is love for self, it's easier to give some of that love away to others and appreciate their effort in their journey.

Last line

If you are contemplating whether or not to marry, do not allow the notion of loneliness to influence your decision, but let the idea alone determine your decision. One may be keeping themselves single for the wrong reasons if they are concerned that something about their personality makes them undeserving of love.

Chapter Seven Summary

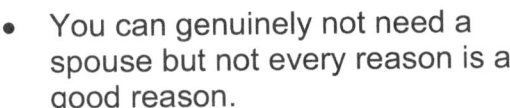

- You can genuinely not need a spouse but not every reason is a good reason.

- You can work on yourself. Don't write yourself off until you succeed.

- People's opinion should not always be a bases for making your decisions.

- Not everyone will like you, but if a lot of people don't like you, look again at yourself before neglecting their opinion.

- You can be alone and not be lonely.

ABOUT THE BOOK

The search for a spouse can be overwhelming for some people. It may become even more challenging for career professionals to balance various aspects of their lives, such as attending to demanding workloads, managing their finances, and juggling friends and family obligations. The purpose of this book is to assist you in selecting the right spouse for yourself.

Toward the end of the book, you are encouraged to ask whether you really need a spouse. There is an excellent reason to ask this question in this time and age as many people search to satisfy the pressure from society. However, when you do not have a compelling reason for wanting a spouse in the first place, the search for one may become a distraction from your goals. Additionally, I discussed some reasons why some people wish to avoid being married and how to approach the issue if this is what you prefer.

As you can imagine, this book is packed with handy tips to help you decide and should be a handy companion for yourself or others you may know who are having difficulties finding love.

ABOUT THE AUTHOR

Ephraim Unuigbe is a chartered accountant and a career and personal finance coach. The author holds a BSc in Accounting, as well as membership in the Institute of Chartered Accountants of Nigeria and certification as a Certified Information Systems Auditor by the Information Systems Audit and Control Association, among other credentials.

Ephraim is currently employed with one of the top accounting firms in the United Kingdom, providing assurance services to corporate entities. Also, Ephraim serves as Director of Corporate Governance on the board of HACTRI (a Nigerian literacy organization). Also, he is a board member of the Itchen Sixth Form College in the United Kingdom.

Ephraim is married to Marian Unuigbe and has two children, Daniel Chukwudi and Eseohen Elizabeth.

ACKNOWLEDGEMENT

To my most important companion, counselor, helper, intercessor, advocate, strengthener, and standby, the Holy Spirit. Thank you.

OTHER BOOKS BY THE AUTHOR TO DATE

- Succeeding in your career - A Roadmap for Graduates & Young Professionals

- Let's talk about money - A guide to Personal Finances for Young Adults

- How to choose a career path - A Spiritual Perspective to Career Choice & Life

- Managing Family Finance - for Career Couples

- The Derailing Youth – For Career Professionals with young adults aged 12 to 19 with absent fathers.

All are available on amazon.com and Ephraim-unuigbe.online

Contact the author via info@ephraim-unuigbe.online.

SERVICES WE OFFER

Career Counselling
We assist individuals of all ages in the clarity and attainment of their career goals, and we also teach students the development of learner-centered skills which they can utilize in their academic careers and life beyond.

Personal Finance Coaching
Personal finance refers to how well people adhere to a budget when managing their finances. Over time, the goal is to save money while also spending money on needed resources and allocating a particular amount for each living expense. With my guidance, you will learn how to make, manage, and multiply your money.

CV Review and Writing
The modern world of employment demands that your CV stands out, and we provide a range of services through which our professional CV writers can create the CV just for you. Every CV we create is tailored specifically to meet your needs.

Cover Letter and Personal Statement
We will provide you with a professional who can write you a high-performing letter for your job application or personal statement. Paired with our professionally written CV, you can differentiate yourself from other applicants.

LinkedIn Profile Optimization

You can take your LinkedIn profile to the next level and turn it into a powerful career tool that highlights your abilities and experiences and impresses your contacts.

Interview Coaching

Our professionals help you be the best candidate your potential employer has ever seen. A well-rounded approach that addresses the verbal and non-verbal factors.

www.ingramcontent.com/pod-product-compliance
Lightning Source LLC
Chambersburg PA
CBHW070245220526
45465CB00004B/1531